Two Minute SQL Server Stumpers

Vol. 6

Brought to you by the staff at
SQLServerCentral.com

And

Red Gate Software

With thanks to everyone who has
contributed to the Question of the Day.

Red Gate Books
Newnham House
Cambridge Business Park
Cambridge
CB4 0WZ
United Kingdom

ISBN 978-1-906434-55-7

Foreword

Why Two Minute Questions?

When I was a kid, I used to order these Scholastic mysteries from the school. They were these little, thin paperbacks, like 50-60 or so pages, much like what you're holding now, that had a short mystery written on a page. Usually they consisted of some story and then a question. How did someone get killed? Where did the murder weapon go? Something like that. You then turned the page to find out the answer after thinking about it for a minute.

We now bring you Volume 6 of our SQL Server Stumpers and, once again, that's what we're trying to build here, but instead of some mystery, it's a quiz type format of SQL Server questions and answers, culled from the annals of our very popular Question of the Day on the SQLServerCentral.com website. These are a collection of questions from the past that we put together to help you study for an exam, learn a bit more about SQL Server, pass the time, etc. But they're mostly collected for…

The INTERVIEW.

You're looking for a new job; you've posted your resume, worked on cover letters, and finally landed an interview. Now you want to be sure that you look your best; that you can answer what's thrown at you.

I can't promise that anyone will ask you any of these questions, but you never know. Maybe some managers that are interviewing will grab a copy of the book and start asking questions out of it. But it will help you prepare, give you some hands on experience, challenge you in a variety of ways about the different aspects of SQL Server. Some of the questions are arcane, some very common, but you'll learn something and the wide range of questions will help you get your mind agile and ready for some quick thinking.

This version is a compilation of SQL Server 2005 and SQL Server 2008 questions, to bring you up to date on the latest version of SQL Server.

So read on, in order, randomly, just start going through them, but do yourself a favor and think about each before turning the page. Challenge yourself and see how well you do.

Thanks for your support and be sure to visit us online.

Steve Jones

SQLServerCentral.com

Question 1

In which type of tree traversal would all nodes at a particular level below the root be traversed before those at lower levels?

Choose one of the answers below:

1. Depth-first traversal

2. Level-oriented traversal

3. English-order traversal

4. Breadth-first traversal.

Answer:

Breadth-first traversal.

Explanation:

Given a tree such as this:

```
        1          / | \        2  3  4
/ \ / \   \    5   6 7  8   9
```

a traversal of nodes in 1-2-3-4-5 order would be a breadth-first traversal.

Ref: Using hierarchyid Data Types -
http://msdn2.microsoft.com/en-us/library/bb677173(SQL.100).aspx

Question 2

In a tree repesentated by the hierarchy id, nodes are shown as /1/, /1/1/, /1/2/, /1/2/3/, etc. In this representation, what would the "2" repesent?

Choose one of the answers below:

1. Nodes at the same level

2. Nodes in the same subtree

3. No particular meaning.

Answer:

2. Nodes in the same subtree

Explanation:

This representation shows the root nodes and the subnodes from each. In this example, the 2's would represent the same subtree in something like this:

    1   / \   1   2   /   /   3

Ref:HierarchyID - http://msdn2.microsoft.com/en-us/library/bb677290(SQL.100).aspx

Question 3

Which of these values is not a valid parameter for IndexProperty?
Choose one of the answers below:

1. IsHypothetical

2. IndexDepth

3. IsUnique

4. IsPrimaryKey

Answer:

4. IsPrimaryKey

Explanation:

The INDEXPROPERTY function allows you to
return various properties of an index. There are many
useful properties, but IsPrimaryKey is not one of
them.

Ref: INDEXPROPERTY -
**http://msdn2.microsoft.com/en-
us/library/ms187729(SQL.100).aspx**

Question 4

Are statistics on data distribution only created for columns that are indexed?

Choose one of the answers below:

      1.   Yes

      2.   No

Answer:

No

Explanation:

If you have the auto_create_statistics option set to ON at the database level, SQL Server will create statistics for columns that are used in predicates even if there is no index on that column.

ref: Index Statistics –
http://msdn2.microsoft.com/en-us/library/ms190397(SQL.100).aspx

Question 5

If you are reading a graphical query plan in SQL Server 2005 and see one of the operators displayed in red, what does this mean?

Choose one of the answers below:

1. There is a warning such as missing statistcs that was reported

2. This operation is being held up by another operator

3. This is a high priority operation.

4. No operators are ever displayed in red.

Answer:

1. There is a warning such as missing statistcs that was reported

Explanation:

Red in a graphical query plan means that the physical operator received a warning, such as out of date or missing statistics. The other options are made up.
Ref: Displaying Graphical Execution Plans

http://msdn2.microsoft.com/en-us/library/ms178071(SQL.100).aspx

Question 6

Can you ensure that you get the actual execution plan SQL Server will use without executing the query?

Choose one of the answers below:

1. No

2. Yes

Answer:

1. No

Explanation:

The Actual execution plan is not provided until you actually execute the query. The estimated plan is all you can get without actually running the query.

Ref: How to: Display an Actual Execution Plan - **http://msdn2.microsoft.com/en-us/library/ms189562(SQL.100).aspx**

Question 7

In SQL Server 2008, which index hint will ensure that in index seek operation is used?

Choose one of the answers below:

1. WITH (INDEX SEEK)

2. WITH (SEEK)

3. WITH (USESEEK)

4. WITH (FORCESEEK)

Answer:

4. WITH (FORCESEEK)

Explanation:

In SQL Server 2008, the FORCESEEK table hint can be used to force the query plan to choose an index seek operation. The others are made up options.

Ref: Using the FORCESEEK Table Hint - **http://msdn2.microsoft.com/en-us/library/bb510478(SQL.100).aspx**

Question 8

What is the default setting for ANSI_NULLs in SQL Server 2005?

Choose one of the answers below:

1. On

2. Off

Answer:

2. Off

Explanation:

By default in SQL Server 2005, ANSI_NULLs are set to Off. You should understand what this means for NULL comparisons and aggregates and knowing the defaults can help your troubleshooting skills.

Ref: Database Options -
http://msdn2.microsoft.com/en-us/library/ms179472.aspx

Question 9

You might have come across this instance of error within your environment:

Msg 18456, Level 14, State 1, Server <ServerName>, Line 1 Login failed for user '<Name>'

Investigating further you look at relevant SQL Server instance error log too for more information on Severity & state of this error. You look at the corresponding as:

2007-05-17 00:12:00.34 Logon Error: 18456, Severity: 14, State: 8.

What is the reason for this error?

Choose one of the answers below:

1. Attempt to use a Windows login name with SQL Authentication

2. Password mismatch

3. Change password required

4. Invalid password

Answer:

2. Password mismatch

Explanation:

See: **http://sqlserver-qa.net/blogs/tools/archive/2007/05/18/msg-18456-level-14-state-1-server-servername-line-1-login-failed-for-user-name.aspx** State 1 is always reported for security purposes. Per Sung Lee Program Manager in SQL Server Protocols (Dev.team) has outlined further information on Error state description: **http://blogs.msdn.com:80/user/Profile.aspx?UserID=11476**

```
  States      Description  2 and 5
Invalid userid     6       Attempt to use
a Windows login name with SQL
Authentication     7       Login disabled
and password mismatch      8
Password mismatch    9        Invalid
password  11 and 12 Valid login but
server access failure    13      SQL
Server service paused    18      Change
password required
```

Question 10

What will be the the the output of following query

SELECT 2 + NULL

Choose one of the answers below:

1. 2

2. Error

Answer:

1. NULL

Explanation:

Since NULL is undefined hence any addition to undefined will be undefined.

Ref: Null Values -
http://msdn2.microsoft.com/en-us/library/ms191504.aspx

Question 11

Which compatibility level is the default for SQL Server 2005?

Choose one of the answers below:

1. 60

2. 70

3. 80

4. 90

5. 10

Answer:

4. 90

Explanation:

SQL Server 2005 is version 9, so the compatibility default is 90. All of these are valid levels, but 90 is the default.

Ref: sp_dbcmptlevel -
http://msdn2.microsoft.com/en-us/library/ms178653.aspx

Question 12

In SQL Server 2005 Analysis Services, what is an additive measure?

Choose one of the answers below:

1. A measure that can be aggregated along one of its dimensions

2. A measure that can be aggregated along one or more, but not all of its dimensions

3. A measure that can be aggregated along all of its dimensions without restrictions

4. A measure that cannot be aggregated along any dimension

Answer:

3. A measure that can be aggregated along all of its dimensions without restrictions

Explanation:

An additive measure is one that can be aggregated along all of its dimensions without any restrictions. There are other terms for the other choices except there is not term for a measure aggregated along only one dimension.

Ref: Configuring Measure Properties - **http://msdn2.microsoft.com/en-us/library/ms175623.aspx**

Question 13

In SQL Server 2005 Analysis Services, can you have a
semiadditive measure if it can be aggregated along a
location dimension, but not the time dimension?

Choose one of the answers below:

1. Yes

2. No

Answer:

1. Yes

Explanation:

A semiadditive measure is one that can be aggregated along some, but not all of its dimensions. So in this case, a measure that can be aggregated along the location, but not the time dimension would be additive. If it were able to be aggregated along all dimensions, it would be additive.

Ref: Configuring Measure Properties - **http://msdn2.microsoft.com/en-us/library/ms175623.aspx**

Question 14

If you had a calculated measure that returned the percentage of sales along some dimension, what type of measure would this be?

Choose one of the answers below:

1. Additive

2. Semiadditive

3. Nonadditive

4. Partial

Answer:

3. Nonadditive

Explanation:

A nonadditive measure is one that cannot be aggregated along any dimension in that group. Percentages are typically nonadditive in that they would not make sense if an aggregation was applied.

Ref: Configuring Measure Properties - **http://msdn2.microsoft.com/en-us/library/ms175623.aspx**

Question 15

What is the output of this expression?

```
select 25 / 5 + 6 * 5
```

Choose one of the answers below:

1. 10

2. 35

3. 55

Answer:

2. 35

Explanation:

The order of operations in this case would place a higher precedence on the multiplication and division than the addition. Therefore the 25/5 would be executed and return 5. 6*5 would be executed and return 30 and then those two results would be added.

Ref: Arithmetic Operators - **http://msdn2.microsoft.com/en-us/library/ms187520.aspx**

Question 16

Which operator has a higher order of precedence in computations?

Choose one of the answers below:

1. Multiplication

2. Division

3. Modulo

4. Multiplication and division are higher than modulo

5. All have the same precedence are executed from left to right.

Answer:

5. All have the same precedence are are executed from left to right.

Explanation:

Of these three operators, multiplication, division, and modulo, they all have the same level of precedence and will be executed from left to right.

Ref: Arithmetic Operators - **http://msdn2.microsoft.com/en-us/library/ms187520.aspx**

Question 17

If you execute a distributed transaction using a linked server and an OLEDB provider, which of these sources can participate in a distributed trasnaction? (select all that apply)

Choose two of the answers below:

1. SQL Server 7.0

2. Access databases

3. Excel spreadsheets

4. Oracle databases

5. Exchange Server

Answer:

1. SQL Server 7.0
4. Oracle databases

Explanation:

Of these, only database services, like Oracle, DB2, or SQL Server, can participate in distributed transactions.

Ref: OLE DB Providers Tested with SQL Server - **http://msdn2.microsoft.com/en-us/library/ms187072.aspx**

Question 18

If you invoke an application role in SQL Server 2005 and wish to issue a query in another database, can the role use permissions granted to the "guest" user in the other database? Assume the application role has not been granted permissions in the other database.

Choose one of the answers below:

1. Yes

2. No

Answer:

1. Yes

Explanation:

An application role exists as a principal in a database like any other user. It uses the permissions of the guest account if it does not have explicit permissions to access a database.

Ref: Application Roles -
http://msdn2.microsoft.com/en-us/library/ms190998.aspx

Question 19

You are testing an application role in SQL Server 2005. You connect with SSMS, invoke the role, and then execute various queries and stored procedures. What can you do to return to your normal account permissions? (select all that apply)

Choose two of the answers below:

1. Disconnect your session and reconnect

2. execute sp_removerole

3. execute sp_unsetapprole

4. execute sp_setapprole with your original credentials.

Answer:

1. Disconnect your session and reconnect
3. execute sp_unsetapprole

Explanation:

When an application role is invoked, it can be removed in only two ways. The first is to disconnect and reconnect with different credentials. The second way is to use sp_unsetapprole. This requires that you have saved information from your original context in a cookie when you invoked the application role.

Ref: Application Roles - **http://msdn2.microsoft.com/en-us/library/ms190998.aspx**

Question 20

Which product will not be available as an RTM today?

Choose one of the answers below:

1. Visual Studio 2008

2. SQL Server 2008

3. Windows 2008

4. All three will RTM today at the Heroes Happen Here Launch

Answer:

2. SQL Server 2008

Explanation:

Sadly, only Visual Studio 2008 and Windows 2008 are available as RTM products today, Feb 27, 2008, at the launch event. SQL Server 2008 will RTM later this year.

Question 21

Certificates be used to encrypt what? (select all that apply)

Choose two of the answers below:

      1.   Symmetric Keys

      2.   Data

      3.   Database Master Keys

Answer:

1. Symmetric Keys
2. Data

Explanation:

Certificates in SQL Server 2005 can be used to encrypt both data and symmetric keys. Database Master Keys are encrypted with the Service Master Key of the instance.

Ref: Encryption Hierarchy - **http://msdn2.microsoft.com/en-us/library/ms190998.aspx**

Question 22

In SQL Server 2005, which of these can be digitally signed?

Choose four of the answers below:

1. Stored Procedures

2. DDL Triggers

3. CLR Assemblies

4. DML Triggers

5. Functions

Answer:

1. Stored Procedures
3. CLR Assemblies
4. DML Triggers
5. Functions

Explanation:

All of these can be digitally signed except DDL triggers.

Ref: Module Signing - **http://msdn2.microsoft.com/en-us/library/ms190998.aspx**

Question 23

In transactional replication, which of the following might increase replication latency?

Choose one of the answers below:

1. "sync with backup" set on both the publisher and distributor

2. "sync with backup" set on the distributor

3. Both of these

4. Neither of these

Answer:

1. "sync with backup" set on both the publisher and distributor

Explanation:

There is a note that setting this on the publisher and distributor will increase latency and your clients must be able to tolerate this.

Reference: - Strategies for Backing Up and Restoring Snapshot and Transactional Replication - **http://msdn2.microsoft.com/en-us/library/ms152560.aspx**

Question 24

If you are moving system databases (master, msdb, model, tempdb), you would change the location of master by changing the startup parameters, bringing down the instance, and moving the master.mdf and master.ldf files.

In SQL Server 2005, how would you move the location of the msdb database?

Choose one of the answers below:

1. Just perform a normal detach and attach as you would for a user database

2. Incorrect Answer

3. Start SQL Server, but not SQL Agent and then perform a detach and attach as you would for a user database.

4. Start SQL Server with -c, -m and -T3608 and then perform a detach. You would then remove these parameters before attaching MSDB.

5. Start SQL Server with -c, -m and -T3608 and then perform a detach and attach as you would for a user database.

Answer:

4. Start SQL Server with -c, -m and -T3608 and then perform a detach. You would then remove these parameters before attaching MSDB.

Explanation:

Moving MSDB is more complicated than other system databases and requires you to add trace flags and parameters to the SQL Server startup to detach msdb, then remove them and restart SQL Server to attach it.

Ref: **http://support.microsoft.com/kb/224071**

Question 25

What is the cause of the following error:

"Too many backup devices specified for restore.Only 64 are allowed.RESTORE HEADERONLY is terminating abnormally."

Choose one of the answers below:

1. Trying to restore a SQL 2005 database onto a SQL 2000 instance

2. SQL Server defaults to the 2000 version of the server

3. Incorrect syntax : RESTORE FILELISTONLY FROM disk = 'C:\sqlbackups\new.bak'

Answer:

1. Trying to restore a SQL 2005 database onto a SQL 2000 instance

Explanation:

It means that the user is logging into the 2000 server instance and since we are trying to restore a higher version of backup to a lower version hence the error.

Question 26

Which of the following does SQL Server 2005 Workgroup Edition **not** support?

Choose one of the answers below:

1. Unlimited database size

2. 64-bit

3. 8Gb RAM

4. Log-shipping

Answer:

3. 8Gb RAM

Explanation:

SQL Server Workgroup Edition only suports up to 3Gb RAM. Database sizes are unlimited. 64-bit support is provided via WOW. Log-shipping is supported.

see -
http://www.microsoft.com/sql/prodinfo/featur es/compare-features.mspx

Question 27

SQL Server 2005 Workgroup Edition does not come with SQL Profiler, however you can still run Profiler against a SQL Server 2005 Workgroup Edition instance.

Choose one of the answers below:

1. TRUE

2. FALSE

Answer:

1. TRUE

Explanation:

Although Profiler is not part of the toolset that gets installed with Workgroup Edition, you can still run Profiler from a Standard or Enterprise install.

Ref: Feature Comparison - **http://www.microsoft.com/sql/prodinfo/featur es/compare-features.mspx**

Question 28

What is the maximum data size (in bytes) of a row in the following table

GCREATE TABLE tbPersonalDetails(
PK_ID INT NOT NULL PRIMARY KEY,
[Name] NVARCHAR(50) NOT NULL,
Married BIT NOT NULL,
DOB SMALLDATETIME NOT NULL,
BachelorsDegree BIT NOT NULL,
MastersDegree BIT NOT NULL,
Profession NVARCHAR(100) NOT NULL,
Retired BIT NOT NULL,
Age AS (DATEDIFF(yy,DOB,GETDATE()))
)
GO

Choose one of the answers below:

1. 162 bytes

2. 159 bytes

3. 309 bytes

4. 420 bytes

Answer:

3. 309 bytes

Explanation:

Up to 8 bit type columns take only 1 byte per row in table. So all bit columns take 1 byte, Name + profession can take max 308 (2 bytes for each NVARCHAR byte, + 2 for the overhead), DOB takes 4, and no space for age column as it is computed column.

Question 29

For an in-place upgrade to SQL Server 2005, which version(s) of SQL Server can used? (Choose three answers)

Choose three of the answers below:

1. SQL Server 2005 RTM or later

2. Only SQL Server 2000 SP 4 or later

3. Only SQL Server 2000 SP 3 or later

4. SQL Server 7.0 SP 4 or later

5. SQL Server 6.5 SP 4 or later

Answer:

1. SQL Server 2005 RTM or later
3. Only SQL Server 2000 SP 3 or later
4. SQL Server 7.0 SP 4 or later

Explanation:

For an in-place upgrade, SQL Server 2005's Setup
program will require that you have certain versions of
either SQL Server 2000 or 7.0. Specifically, you can
use the in-place method provided by SQL Server
2005 Setup to directly upgrade the following versions:
" SQL Server 7.0 Service Pack 4 (SP4) or later " SQL
Server 2000 SP3, SP4, or later " SQL Server 2005
RTM or later SQL Server 6.5 databases and instances
cannot be directly upgraded and must be manually
upgraded. SQL Server 2005 Upgrade Technical
Reference Guide, page 7
**http://www.microsoft.com/downloads/details.a
spx?FamilyID=3d5e96d9-0074-46c4-bd4f-
c3eb2abf4b66&DisplayLang=en**

Question 30

Given a "date of birth" value as a datetime type, what is the best way to calculate the current age (in years, as a tinyint value)?

Choose one of the answers below:

1. DATEDIFF(yy, DateOfBirth, GETDATE())

2. FLOOR(CONVERT(decimal(9, 2), DATEDIFF(d, DateOfBirth, GETDATE())) / 365.0)

3. DATEDIFF(yy, DateOfBirth, GETDATE()) - CASE WHEN DATEPART(m, DateOfBirth) >= DATEPART(m, GETDATE()) AND DATEPART(d, DateOfBirth) >= DATEPART(d, GETDATE()) THEN 0 ELSE 1 END

Answer:

3. DATEDIFF(yy, DateOfBirth, GETDATE()) -
CASE WHEN DATEPART(m, DateOfBirth) >=
DATEPART(m, GETDATE()) AND
DATEPART(d, DateOfBirth) >= DATEPART(d,
GETDATE()) THEN 0 ELSE 1 END

Explanation:

The first answer, "DATEDIFF(yy, DateOfBirth,
GETDATE())", is very efficient and readable, but
what you have to remember about the DATEDIFF()
function is that it first parses the specified
DATEPART() from each value, then takes the
difference of those. The incorrect expectation is to
think it calculates the difference of the values first (to
the highest precision available), and then returns that
difference as specified by the DATEPART. So the
first answer would actually return the person's age at
the end of the year. The second answer,
"FLOOR(CONVERT(decimal(9, 2), DATEDIFF(d,
DateOfBirth, GETDATE())) / 365.0)", is far more
accurate, because it calculates the difference in days
and then divides by 365. This is roughly correct, but
doesn't account for leap years, and thus might be off
by a handful of days. The third answer first gets the
difference in years, then subtracts 1 if the person has
not yet had a birthday this year. This answer is 100%
accurate, and is the correct response.

Question 31

Which of these is indicates ain incorrect password?
(choose all the apply)

Choose one of the answers below:

1. Login failed for user 'Jim'.

2. Login failed for user 'MyDomain\Jim'.

Answer:

1. Login failed for user 'Jim'.

Explanation:

Only the first one of these is indicative of a password problem. Passwords are only used when SQL Authentication is used in the login. The second error indicates that the domain user has not been granted rights to connect to SQL Server.

Ref: SQL Server 2005: How to debug login failures (18456, anyone?) - **http://blogs.msdn.com/lcris/archive/2008/02/21/sql-server-2005-how-to-debug-login-failures-18456-anyone.aspx**

Question 32

Which version of SQL Server 2005 is fully compatible with Windows Vista and the 2007 Microsoft Office system?

Choose one of the answers below:

    1. SQL Server 2005 RTM

    2. SQL Server 2005 SP 1

    3. SQL Server 2005 SP 2

Answer:

3. SQL Server 2005 SP 2

Explanation:

SQL Server Service Pack 2 or greater is needed to be fully compatible with Windows Vista and Microsoft Office 2007.

Ref: SQL Server 2005 Service Pack 2 Web Site - **http://technet.microsoft.com/en-us/sqlserver/bb426877.aspx**

Question 33

You have a table EMPLOYEE that has 50 columns. You are the DBA and in a test environment you are looking at some data. You issue the T-SQL command

select * from employee

and get all the rows returned, but something catches your keen DBA eye, and you want to explore further. You are interested in the employee starting dates and want to see them in order so you change your query to

select start_date, * from employee order by start_date desc

(You can assume that the table exists and contains a column named start_date)What is the result of running this command?

Choose one of the answers below:

1. All columns and all rows from the employee table in descending start_date order, with the start_date as the first column

2. All columns and all rows from the employee table in descending start_date order, with the start_date as the last column

3. An error : Msg 209, Level 16, State 1 - Ambiguous column name 'start_date'

4. An error : Incorrect syntax near '*'

Answer:

3. An error : Msg 209, Level 16, State 1 - Ambiguous column name 'start_date'

Explanation:

In the ORDER BY clause, 'start_date' is an expression, which in this case directly represents a column name, but it is not unique as 'start_date' will also be included as part of the * in the SELECT statement. To get round this, qualify the column names in the ORDER BY clause: select start_date, * from employee order by employee.start_date desc

Question 34

What are the possible causes of the error , when you build or update the OLAP cube database (select all that apply):

Analysis Services session failed with the following error: Failed to connect to the Analysis Services server <AnalysisServicesServerName>. Error: ActiveX component can't create object

Choose three of the answers below:

1. Microsoft SQL Server Native Client not installed

2. Microsoft SQL Server 2005 Management Objects Collection not installed

3. Microsoft SQL Server 2005 Backward Compatibility Components not installed

Answer:

1. Microsoft SQL Server Native Client not installed
2. Microsoft SQL Server 2005 Management Objects Collection not installed
3. Microsoft SQL Server 2005 Backward Compatibility Components not installed

Explanation:

Possible causes:
Three SQL Server 2005 Analysis Services components must be installed on the Project Server application server. If all of them are not installed, then this error occurs.

SQL Server 2005 Analysis Services components must be installed to the Project Server application server.

Microsoft SQL Server Native Client (sqlncli.msi)

Microsoft SQL Server 2005 Management Objects Collection (sqlserver2005_xmo.msi)

Microsoft SQL Server 2005 Backward Compatibility Components (SQLServer2005_BC.msi)

Question 35

How do you enable the CLR in SQL Server 2005 ?

Choose one of the answers below:

1. sp_configure 'clr enabled', 1 GO
   RECONFIGURE GO

2. sp_configure 'clr enabled', 0 GO
   RECONFIGURE GO

3. sp_configure 'clr enabled', 1

Answer:

1. sp_configure 'clr enabled', 1 GO RECONFIGURE GO

Explanation:

CLR in SQL Server 2005 can be enabled by doing the following: sp_configure 'clr enabled', 1 GO RECONFIGURE GO

Ref: Enable CLR Integration - **http://msdn2.microsoft.com/en-us/library/ms254506.aspx** Ref:

Question 36

How much information does a Yottabyte store?
(check all that apply)

Choose two of the answers below:

1. 1024^8

2. 10^{24}

3. 1000^8

4. 2^{80}

Answer:

2. 10^24
3. 1000^8

Explanation:

A yottabyte is 10^24th or (10^3)^8. This is one septillion, slightly less than yobibyte YiB (2^80).

Reference: **http://en.linuxreviews.org/Yottabyte**

Question 37

What is the condition to be used to extract records of the employees joined in the month of Jan, Feb, March, April, May, Aug from table employee having a field of join_date? (select all that apply)

Choose two of the answers below:

1. month(join_date) in (1,2,3,4,5,8)

2. datename(m,join_date) like '%a%'

3. Not in List

Answer:

1. month(join_date) in (1,2,3,4,5,8)
2. datename(m,join_date) like '%a%'

Explanation:

Either of the first two answers will work. All the month names have at least the letter 'a' once. The month function returns the number of the month, that can be compared against the month number of given months

Question 38

Is there any other way to extract the details about the students born in the month of Feb, June, July, Aug, Nov, Dec - from the table stud_mast other than using the IN and OR operators? Ex. select * from stud_mast where month(dob) in (2,6,7,8,11,12)

Choose one of the answers below:

1. Yes

2. No

3. Given Query itself is incorrect

Answer:

1. Yes

Explanation:

Yes. Because all the months here specified will have the odd number of characters, so we can use the condition in where clause as len(datename(m,dob))%2=1

% : modulo operator , x % y => returns the remainder when x is divided by y

Ref: Modulo - **http://msdn2.microsoft.com/en-us/library/aa276866(SQL.80).aspx**

Question 39

Using Transact-SQL, how can you find out whether SQLAgent is running? (Select all that apply)

Choose two of the answers below:

    1.   Query sysprocesses table for program_name like SQLAgent%

    2.   Use xp_servicecontrol querystate SQLSERVERAGENT

    3.   use sp_services SQLAgent

Answer:

1. Query sysprocesses table for program_name like SQLAgent%
2. Use xp_servicecontrol querystate SQLSERVERAGENT

Explanation:

Querying the sysprocesses table will return a row if sql agent is running, else it will not return any rows. The xp_servicecontrol procedure will return the status of the service (running/stopped) on 2005 / 2008 editions except express. On a SQL Server Express instance this command will return an error. So you need to check for errors as well as the status to determine whether the agent is running.

Question 40

Is there a condition for the WHERE clause to display the details about the students born in the month numbers of 1[Jan], 3,4,5,7,8? The condition should not use both IN and OR operators.

Choose one of the answers below:

1. No

2. Yes

3. Not Supported in SQL Server

Answer:

2. Yes

Explanation:

We can give the condition as follows:

where datename(m,dob) not like '%e%'

because these month(s) specified do not have the letter 'e', but all the other months have at least one 'e' in month name.

Question 41

SQL Server 2008 is going open source to compete with MySQL and PostgreSQL!

Choose one of the answers below:

   1.   TRUE

   2.   FALSE

Answer:

2. FALSE

Explanation:

April Fools and there is no chance that SQL Server is going Open Source anytime soon!

Question 42

Someone requests an adhoc full backup of your Sales database to be used for a reporting server. There is currently a scheduled full backup running right now. Can you start a second full backup running in SQL Server 2005?

Choose one of the answers below:

1. Yes

2. No

Answer:

2. No

Explanation:

There are some administrative tasks that can execute simultaneously, but two full backups running concurrently are not allowed:

Ref: Concurrent Administrative Operations - **http://msdn2.microsoft.com/en-us/library/ms189315.aspx**

Question 43

There is a backup log task occurring and it is expected to take 20 minutes to clear out a stuck transaction. Someone asks if you can quickly run a full backup to use for reporting purposes since full backups normally take about 10 minutes. Can you start a full backup in SQL Server 2005 when a log backup is running?

Choose one of the answers below:

1. Yes

2. No

Answer:

1. Yes

Explanation:

A full backup can be run simultaneously with a log backup, however not all administrative tasks can be done concurrently.

Ref: Concurrent Administrative Tasks - **http://msdn2.microsoft.com/en-us/library/ms189315.aspx**

Question 44

How many Dedicated Adminstrator Connectiosn can you have concurrently on a SQL Server 2005 instance?

Choose one of the answers below:

> **1.** 1
>
> **2.** 2 if one is local
>
> **3.** 2 and both can be remote
>
> **4.** 8

Answer:

1. 1

Explanation:

Only one DAC connection is allowed on each SQL Server 2005 instance at a time. Subsequent connection requests as a DAC connection are denied with error 17810.

Ref: Dedicated Administrator Connection - **http://msdn2.microsoft.com/en-us/library/ms189595.aspx**

Question 45

Does SQL Server 2005 Express allow Dedicated
Administrator Connections (DAC)?

Choose one of the answers below:

1. Yes, always

2. Yes, if remote connections are allowed.

3. Yes, if started with trace flag 7806

4. No

Answer:

3. Yes, if started with trace flag 7806

Explanation:

SQL Server 2005 Express Edition does not listen on the DAC port by default. If it is started with trace flag 7806, then DAC connections can be made.

Ref: Using a Dedicated Administrator Connection - **http://msdn2.microsoft.com/en-us/library/ms189595.aspx**

Question 46

On which port can you make a Dedicated Administrator Connection (DAC)?

Choose one of the answers below:

1. 1435

2. 3389

3. 1433

4. Dynamically assigned

Answer:

4. Dynamically assigned

Explanation:

The DAC port is dynamically assigned when the instance starts and listed in the SQL Server error log. By default it tries for 1434, but it is possible that this port is already in use. The message will be something like:

```
  Dedicated admin connection support was
established for listening locally on port
1977.
```

Ref: Using a Dedicated Administrator Connection - **http://msdn2.microsoft.com/en-us/library/ms189595.aspx**

Question 47

In SQL Server 2005, which command would you use to make a tail log backup of the Sales database prior to restoring it?

Choose one of the answers below:

1. BACKUP LOG Sales to Disk = 'c:\sales.log' with norecovery

2. BACKUP LOG Sales to Disk = 'c:\sales.log' with tail

3. BACKUP TAIL LOG Sales to Disk = 'c:\sales.log' with norecovery

4. There is no way to make a tail log backup

Answer:

1. BACKUP LOG Sales to Disk = 'c:\sales.log' with norecovery

Explanation:

A tail-log backup is like any other backup. If the database is online, you can issue the regular log backup command with NORECOVERY added to it. If the database is damanged, then you can try the NO_TRUNCATE or CONTINUE_AFTER_ERROR options instead.

Ref: Tail-Log Backups - **http://msdn2.microsoft.com/en-us/library/ms179314.aspx**

Question 48

In SQL Server 2005, how would you rebuild a damaged master database?

Choose one of the answers below:

1. Run rebuildm.exe

2. Run the setup program from the Command Prompt and add the REBUILDDATABASE parameter.

3. Right click the master database from SSMS and select REBUILD

4. Run the GUI setup program from your original CD and select Rebuild System Databases

Answer:

2. Run the setup program from the Command Prompt and add the REBUILDDATABASE parameter.

Explanation:

Rebuildm.exe has been discontinued in SQL Server 2005. Instead you must run setup from the command prompt and add the REBUILDDATABASE parameter.

Ref: Rebuilding the master Database - **http://msdn2.microsoft.com/en-us/library/ms191431.aspx**

Question 49

If you rebuild the master database in SQL Server 2005, what happens to your version level?

Choose one of the answers below:

1. It reverts to the RTM version, losing service packs and additonal patches

2. It reverts to the latest Service Pack version, losing any additional patches.

3. It remains the same.

Answer:

1. It reverts to the RTM version, losing service packs and additonal patches

Explanation:

When you rebuild the master database, all system databases, including the systemresource database, are rebuilt from original media, so all Service Pack, Hotfix, QFE/GDR information is lost and you revert to the original RTM version.

Ref: How to: Install SQL Server 2005 from the Command Prompt (scroll down to rebuild database section) - **http://msdn2.microsoft.com/en-us/library/ms144259.aspx**

Question 50

In SQL Server 2005, how do you perform a backup using Named Pipes?

Choose one of the answers below:

1. Normal backups to local disks all use named pipes

2. In the TO part of the backup command, specify the pipe as "TO PIPE = '\sql\pipe'"

3. SQL Server 2005 does not support backup to named pipes.

Answer:

3. SQL Server 2005 does not support backup to named pipes.

Explanation:

In SQL Server 2005, the ability to backup to a named pipe (disk or tape) was removed.

Ref: Discontinued Database Engine Functionality in SQL Server 2005 - **http://msdn2.microsoft.com/en-us/library/ms144262.aspx**

Question 51

Can you upgrade SQL Server 2005 Evaluation Edition to the full version of SQL Server 2005?

Choose one of the answers below:

1. No, you must uninstall and reinstall

2. Yes, but only to the Enterprise Edition of SQL Server 2005

3. Yes, to all other editions.

Answer:

3. Yes, to all other editions.

Explanation:

You can upgrade the evaluation edition to any other edition without uninstalling.

Ref: Version and Edition Upgrades - **http://msdn2.microsoft.com/en-us/library/ms143393.aspx**

Question 52

I have 3 UPDATE triggers on a individual table, TRA, TRB and TRC. Can I fire them in the sequence TRA, TRB and TRC?

Choose one of the answers below:

1. No

2. Yes

Answer:

2. Yes

Explanation:

http://msdn2.microsoft.com:80/en-us/library/ms186762.aspx Using sp_settriggerorder

Set TRA as first, TRC as LAST and TRB will fire between TRA and TRC firing which is what is desired.

Question 53

In SQL Server 2005, how can you easily determine which columns have the identity property set? (select all that apply).

Choose two of the answers below:

1. Query sys.identity_columns for the rows.

2. Query sys.tables.identity_column for the name of the column in each table

3. Query sys.columns.is_identity for a value of 1

4. There is no way to do this in T-SQL.

Answer:

1. Query sys.identity_columns for the rows.
3. Query sys.columns.is_identity for a value of 1

Explanation:

There is a table, sys.identity_columns that contains a row for each column in your database that has the identity property set. There is also a column called is_identity in the sys.columns view that contains a 1 if the column has the identity property set. The other answer was made up.

Ref: sys.identity_columns - **http://msdn2.microsoft.com/en-us/library/ms187334.aspx**

Question 54

What would be the output of the below script?

```
CREATE TABLE #myTable (column1 text);  GO
INSERT INTO #myTable VALUES ('test');  GO
SELECT BINARY_CHECKSUM(*) from
#myTable;  GO  DROP TABLE #myTable  GO
```

Choose one of the answers below:

1. Return a int value

2. Error in binarychecksum. There are no comparable columns in the binarychecksum input.

3. We cannot use Binary Checksum with temporary tables

Answer:

2. Error in binarychecksum. There are no comparable columns in the binarychecksum input.

Explanation:

BINARY_CHECKSUM ignores columns of noncomparable data types in its computation. Noncomparable data types include text, ntext, image, cursor, xml, and noncomparable common language runtime (CLR) user-defined types.

Ref: Binary_checksum - **http://msdn.microsoft.com/en-us/library/ms173784.aspx**

Question 55

What is the output of this query?

  select floor(13.890)

Choose one of the answers below:

      1.   14

      2.   13.9

      3.   13

Answer:

3. 13

Explanation:

Floor returns the largest integer less than or equal to the specified numeric expression. In this case, that is 13.

Ref: Floor - **http://msdn2.microsoft.com/en-us/library/ms178028.aspx**

Question 57

What would you use to update a single table's statistics in the shortest time?

Choose one of the answers below:

1. sp_updatestats

2. UPDATE STATISTICS

3. All of the above

Answer:

2. UPDATE STATISTICS

Explanation:

Sp_updatestats does not have an option to update a single table's statistic. It will update all tables in the database. This answer is incorrect. UPDATE STATISTICS can be used with single table and therefore it will run in most cases faster.

Ref: UPDATE STATISTICS - **http://msdn2.microsoft.com/en-us/library/aa260645(SQL.80).aspx**

Question 58

Which registry key houses the values for the name of SQL Server 2005's installed instances?

Choose one of the answers below:

1. HKLM\SOFTWARE\Microsoft\Microsoft SQL Native Client

2. HKLM\SOFTWARE\Microsoft\Microsoft SQL Server

3. HKLM\SOFTWARE\Microsoft\Microsoft SQL Server 2005 Redist

Answer:

2. HKLM\SOFTWARE\Microsoft\Microsoft SQL Server

Explanation:

The "InstalledInstance" Value is located in HKLM\SOFTWARE\Microsoft\Microsoft SQL Server.

Question 59

Which of the three lines will correctly remove duplicated items in the following table:

Create table #new(ID int null, Keyvalue varchar(2))

insert into #new(id,keyvalue) values (1,'aa')

insert into #new(id,keyvalue) values (2,'bb')

insert into #new(id,keyvalue) values (1,'aa')

insert into #new(id,keyvalue) values (1,'aa')

Choose one of the answers below:

1. with numbered;(SELECT rowno=row_number() over (partition by ID order by ID),ID,keyvalue from #new)delete from numbered where rowno>1

2. ;with numbered as(SELECT rowno=row_number() over (partition by ID order by ID),ID,keyvalue from #new)delete from numbered where rowno>1

3. ;with numbered as(SELECT rowno=row_number() over (partition by ID order by ID),ID,keyvalue from #new)delete from numbered where rowno=1

Answer:

2. ;with numbered as(SELECT
rowno=row_number() over (partition by ID order by
ID),ID,keyvalue from #new)delete from numbered
where rowno>1

Explanation:

Of these statements, the first one produces a syntax
error. The last one produces a table with 2 duplicates.
The second one is correct. A semi-colon at the
beginning of the statement is valid and we want to
delete all the matching row numbers greater than 1.

Question 60

In SQL Server 2005, a strored procedure can return the data using: (select all that apply)

Choose three of the answers below:

1. Output parameter

2. Return Code

3. Cursor data type in an output parameter

Answer:

1. Output parameter
2. Return Code
3. Cursor data type in an output parameter

Explanation:

The stored procedure can return the data using output parameters, a return code and as well as a cursor data type.

Ref: Designing Stored Procedures -
http://msdn2.microsoft.com/en-us/library/ms191132.aspx

Question 61

What happens with this code?

    select 'B' union   select 4

Choose one of the answers below:

> **1.** The int is converted to varchar
>
> **2.** The varchar is converted in int (error results)
>
> **3.** The query does not compile.

Answer:

2. The varchar is converted in int (error results)

Explanation:

This is an example of an implicit conversion. In this case, an error is returned as the varchar is converted to an int, or an attempt is made, which returns an error. The int is of higher precedence than a varchar, so that is the order of conversions.

Ref: Connect and Implicit Casts -
http://blogs.msdn.com/isaac/archive/2008/04/10/connect-and-implicit-casts.aspx
Data Type Precedence -
http://msdn2.microsoft.com/en-us/library/ms190309%28SQL.100%29.aspx

Question 62

With the user defined function in SQL Server 2005:

```
 CREATE FUNCTION
[dbo].[fn_DoSomething](@Bin VARCHAR(10))
RETURNS VARCHAR(12)
AS
BEGIN
 DECLARE @L AS INT
 SET @L = LEN(LTRIM(RTRIM(@Bin)))
 RETURN (@Bin)
END
GO
```

What value would you expect to be returned when executing this code in SQL Server 2005?

```
SELECT dbo.fn_DoSomething('1234567890ABC')
```

Choose one of the answers below:

1. An error message

2. 1234567890AB

3. 1234567890

4. 1234567890ABC

Answer:

3. 1234567890

Explanation:

Try it to see for yourself. It will return "1234567890" and this appears to be a glitch in SQL 2005 at compatibility level 90 and in SQL 2000.

Question 63

The AdventureWorks database has the HumanResources.Employee table with a column SalariedFlag defined as follows:

[SalariedFlag] [dbo].[Flag] NOT NULL
The Flag user-defined data type is defined by:
CREATE TYPE [dbo].[Flag] FROM [bit] NOT NULL

What will be the result when the following query is executed on SQL Server 2005?

USE AdventureWorks
SELECT COUNT(*) as [Number of Salaried Employees]
FROM HumanResources.Employee
WHERE SalariedFlag = 'true'

Choose one of the answers below:

1. A numeric result will be returned.

2. An error message will appear: Syntax error converting the varchar value 'true' to a column of data type bit.

3. A result set with no value (a blank result) will be returned.

Answer:

1. A numeric result will be returned.

Explanation:

In SQL Server 2005, the string values TRUE and FALSE can be converted to bit values. See the SQL Server Books Online topic "bit (Transact-SQL)" at **http://msdn2.microsoft.com/en-us/library/ms177603.aspx**.

In SQL Server 2000, a query such as: USE Northwind; SELECT * FROM Products WHERE discontinued = 'true'; would give the error message.

Question 64

How can you enable FILESTREAM in SQL Server 2008?

Choose one of the answers below:

1. sp_filestream_configure

2. xp_cmdshell

3. xp_filestream_configure

4. sp_cmdshell

Answer:

1. sp_filestream_configure

Explanation:

For enabling FILESTREAM storage in SQL Server 2008 one needs to execute sp_filestream_configure with parameter @enable_level set to 1, 2, or 3.

Ref: sp_filestream_configure -
http://msdn2.microsoft.com/en-us/library/bb934198(SQL.100).aspx

Question 65

What is the purpose of FILESTREAM storage in SQL Server 2008?

Choose one of the answers below:

1. To enable user direct access to database files

2. To store BLOB data on file system

3. To allow network storage of data and log files

Answer:

2. To store BLOB data on file system

Explanation:

FILESTREAM storage allows user to create a table with a varbinary(max) column (BLOB) which is actually stored on the filesystem, rather than as a field in the row.

Ref: Designing and Implementing FILESTREAM - **http://msdn2.microsoft.com/en-us/library/bb895234(SQL.100).aspx**

Question 66

How do you know whether FILESTREAM storage is available and enabled in SQL Server 2008?

Choose one of the answers below:

1. Query Sys,Configurations view for 'FileStreamAccessLevel'

2. Query the Sys.assembly_files for 'FileStream'

3. Query the server property 'FilestreamEffectiveLevel'

Answer:

3. Query the server property
'FilestreamEffectiveLevel'

Explanation:

For knowing the current effective level of FileStream access you need to run the following query –

  SELECT SERVERPROPERTY
('FilestreamShareName')   ,SERVERPROPERTY
('FilestreamEffectiveLevel');
which will give you the instance name and the filestream access level. If the level is set to 3 the filestream storage is enabled and available.

Ref: sp_filestream_configure -
**http://msdn2.microsoft.com/en-
us/library/bb934198(SQL.100).aspx**

Question 67

The database user or SQL Server login is impersonated when the EXECUTE AS statement is executed or specified in a module. Which of the following statements are true about the impersonation? (Select all that apply)

Choose two of the answers below:

1. Another EXECUTE AS statement or the REVERT statement must be used before the impersonation will end.

2. The database user or SQL Server login impersonation ends when the session is dropped or when the module finishes its execution.

3. If the statement is called by a member of sysadmin, server-level impersonation is used. If the statement is called by an account that is dbo, database-level impersonation is used.

4. The scope of the impersonation is explicitly defined

Answer:

2. The database user or SQL Server login impersonation ends when the session is dropped or when the module finishes its execution.
4. The scope of the impersonation is explicitly defined

Explanation:

Although using another Execute As statement or the revert statement will modify the impersonation it is not necessary to execute either statement to end the impersonation. The impersonation will end automatically when the session is dropped or the module completes its execution.

Ref: Understanding Context Switching - **http://msdn2.microsoft.com/en-us/library/ms191296.aspx** The scope of the impersonation is explicitly defined in the Execute AS statement. The SETUSER statement is implicit. http://msdn2.microsoft.com/en-us/library/ms188315.aspx

Question 68

What will happen if following query get executed:

select CategoryID, Quantity, Price
from Customer c, SalesOrderDetail sod
where sod.clientid in (select customerid where
pricingplan='X')

Choose one of the answers below:

1. Query will return error because the
   From clause is missing in query used in
   where clause

2. Query will succeed if the customerid
   column is available in any table used in
   the first From Clause

3. Query is wrong

Answer:

2. Query will succeed if the customerid column is available in any table used in the first From Clause

Explanation:

If any attribute is available in the outer From Clause then it will validate column in that before returning any error. You can view this with the following code:

```
  create table customer (ClientID int,
customername varchar(10), pricingplan
char(1))  --create table customer
(ClientID int, customername varchar(10),
pricingplan char(1), CustomerID int)   go
create table SalesOrderDetail (ClientID
int, CustomerName varchar(10), categoryid
int, quantity int, price money,
customerid int)  go  insert customer
select 1, 'Steve', 'X'  insert customer
select 2, 'Andy', 'Y'  -- insert customer
select 1, 'Steve', 'X', 1  -- insert
customer select 2, 'Andy', 'Y', 2  insert
SalesOrderDetail select 1, 'Steve', 1, 2,
10, 1  insert SalesOrderDetail select 2,
'Andy', 1, 5, 10, 2    select CategoryID,
Quantity, Price  from Customer c,
SalesOrderDetail sod  where sod.clientid
in (select customerid where
pricingplan='X')    drop table Customer
drop table SalesOrderDetail
```

You can also remove CustomerID from both tables and see that it causes an error.

Question 69

You have a default SQL2000 SP4 install.

select * from sysprocesses

reports SPID 55 as blocking SPID 55. You also notice that the waitime value is low and the waittype is a latch waittype

What is the most likely reason?

Choose one of the answers below:

1. The code has entered into an infinite loop, blocking itself

2. As of SP4, sysprocesses reports latch waits and the behaviour is expected

3. Parallelism is enabled and the SPID is waiting for other threads of the SPID to finish

4. SPID 55 is reserved for CHECKPOINTS and is waiting for the next CHECKPOINT interval

Answer:

2. As of SP4, sysprocesses reports latch waits and the behaviour is expected

Explanation:

After you install Microsoft SQL Server 2000 Service Pack 4 (SP4), you may notice that the blocked column in the sysprocesses system table is populated for latch waits in addition to lock waits. Sometimes, you may notice brief periods of time when a single server process ID (SPID) is reported as blocking itself. This behavior is expected.

Ref: KB 906344
http://support.microsoft.com/default.aspx/kb/906344

Question 70

You have a default SQL2005 SP2 install. What is the
output from the following

 set language us_english set dateformat dmy go
declare @date datetime set @date = '11 apr 2008
17:10' select left(@date,1)

Choose one of the answers below:

 1. 1

 2. 4

 3. A

 4. An error 'The conversion of a char
 data type to a datetime data type
 resulted in an out-of-range datetime
 value.'

Answer:

3. A

Explanation:

The default conversion of a date type to character data is style 0, 'mon dd yyyy hh:miAM (or PM)', which gives us 'Apr 11 2008 5:10PM' and the left function returns the leftmost n characters, in this case 1 character, namely 'A'. Setting the DATEFORMAT to DMY has no impact on the outcome, as this setting is used only in the interpretation of character strings as they are converted to date values.

Ref:SET DATEFORMAT - **http://msdn2.microsoft.com/en-us/library/ms189491(SQL.100).aspx**

Question 71

First question of day: what is the len of @c?
declare @c varchar(8000)

set @c = N'hello' + replicate('-',8000)
print len(@c)
print @c

Choose one of the answers below:

1. 8000

2. 4000

3. 2000

Answer:

2. 4000

Explanation:

The CAST to NVARCHAR(4000) means that the maximum len is 4000, then the cast to varchar(8000) allows more characters, but the string is already truncated.

Ref: CAST and CONVERT - **http://msdn2.microsoft.com/en-us/library/ms187928.aspx**

Question 72

Second question of day: what is the len of @c?

declare @c varchar(800)

set @c = N'hello' + replicate('-',800)
print len(@c)
print @c

Choose one of the answers below:

1. 800

2. 400

3. 4000

Answer:

1. 800

Explanation:

The CAST to nvarchar(800) has a maximum 4000 character len. The CAST then to varchar(800) fits in that space, so the len is 800

Ref: CAST and CONVERT - http://msdn2.microsoft.com/en-us/library/ms187928.aspx

Question 73

What do you expect the result of the following query to be? No cheating, don't run until you've answered!
WITH DATA (Numbers) AS
(SELECT NULL UNION ALL
SELECT NULL UNION ALL
SELECT NULL UNION ALL
SELECT 1 UNION ALL
SELECT 2 UNION
SELECT 3)
SELECT COUNT(ALL Numbers) AS
NULLNumberCount FROM DATA
WHERE Numbers IS NULL

Choose one of the answers below:

1. 0

2. 1

3. 3

4. 6

Answer:

2. 0

Explanation:

The final UNION negates the duplicates selected with the previous UNION ALL statements. The COUNT(ALL expression) evaluates the expression for each row in a group and returns the number of nonnull values. ALL Applies the aggregate function to all values. ALL is the default.

For investigation, change the final UNION to UNION ALL, and the SELECT COUNT (ALL Numbers) to COUNT (*)

Ref: COUNT - **http://msdn2.microsoft.com/en-us/library/ms180026.aspx**
COUNT - **http://msdn2.microsoft.com/en-us/library/ms175997.aspx**

Question 74

Ever want or need a very much smaller version of your massive SQL 2005 production database where you could examine the execution plans for slow running queries, modify them and check for improvements, create new SPs and check execution plans all without tying up or bogging down your production environment? You do? Then create a clone. Which of these statements about cloning is true in SQL Server?

Choose one of the answers below:

1. Creating a clone is not legal

2. Create a clone for testing

3. Clone is not efficient

Answer:

2. Create a clone for testing

Explanation:

From a public blog - so owners permission to use is assumed –

http://sqlblog.com/blogs/kalen_delaney/archiv e/2007/11/21/cloning-in-sql-server-2005.aspx

Question 75

How many pages are allocated to a log file in a database with a 10MB log?

Choose one of the answers below:

      1.   1280

      2.   160

      3.   0

Answer:

3. 0

Explanation:

Zero. Log files contain log records, not pages.

Reference: Pages and Extents -
**http://msdn2.microsoft.com/en-
us/library/ms190969.aspx**

Question 76

What information is stored in the sys.dm_clr_tasks DMV?

Choose one of the answers below:

1. A row for each assembly that has been added to the datbase

2. A row for each function in the database that has a CLR reference in its code.

3. A row for each task that is running a batch containin a CLR task

4. This DMV does not exist in SQL Server 2005

Answer:

3. A row for each task that is running a batch containin a CLR task

Explanation:

The sys.dm_clr_tasks contains a row for each CLR task that is executing. Each batch containing a reference to CLR code creates a task and all CLR items in that batch execute under that task.

Ref: sys.dm_clr_rasks -
http://msdn2.microsoft.com/en-us/library/ms177528.aspx

Question 77

The sys.dm_db_mirroring_connections DMV contains rows for each connection made by database mirroring processes. In the login_state column there are various values that describe how the connection is made. The values are numeric and each coresponds to a type of authentication. Which of these is not valid? (select all that apply)

Choose one of the answers below:

1. Arbitration

2. SSPI

3. SQLAuth

4. PublicKeyLogin

5. Negotiate

Answer:

3. SQLAuth

Explanation:

Of these answers, only SQLAuth is not a valid item. The list is

      1. Initial

      2. Negotiate

      3. SSPI

      4. PublicKeyLogin

      5. PublicKeyTentative

      6. LoggedIn

      7. Arbitration

Ref: sys.dm_db_mirroring_connections - **http://msdn2.microsoft.com/en-us/library/ms189796.aspx**

Question 78

In SQL Server 2005 Database Mirroring, which form is used to specify the network address of the servers? (items inside brackets are replaced with your specifics)

Choose one of the answers below:

1. tcp://<server address>:<port>

2. http://<server address>:<endpoint name>

3. dbm://<server address>:<port>

4. udp://<server address>:<port>

Answer:

1. tcp://<server address>:<port>

Explanation:

The server address in Database Mirroring is specified with the TCP start, followed by colon and two slashes before the server address and port are specified, separated by a colon. The port must correspond to the endpoint on the other server that has been setup for database mirroring.

Ref: Specifying a Server Network Address (Database Mirroring) - **http://msdn2.microsoft.com/en-us/library/ms189921.aspx**

Question 79

Given the following script -

create table #fun(id int identity(1,1) primary key
clustered, crit int)

insert #fun(crit)
select top 250000 rand(checksum(newid()))* 10
from syscolumns sc1, syscolumns sc2
--select statement #1
select count(*) from #fun
where crit between 3 and 5

--select statement #2
select count(*) from #fun
where crit between 5 and 3

Would statements #1 and #2 consistently return the
same result set?

Choose one of the answers below:

      1.   Yes

      2.   No

      3.   Can't be determined

Answer:

2. No

Explanation:

In plain language, BETWEEN is a commutative operation, so the order in which you specify the criteria is irrelevant.

In TransactSQL, however, BETWEEN is not communtative. Books Online defines BETWEEN as:

"BETWEEN returns TRUE if the value of test_expression is greater than or equal to the value of begin_expression and less than or equal to the value of end_expression."

By that definition, there is no attempt to reorder the parameters, so Statement #2 will always return 0.

For more info on BETWEEN - **http://msdn.microsoft.com/en-us/library/ms187922.aspx**

Question 80

In SQL Server 2005, using the following query to access sys.dm_exec_query_stats;

  SELECT [Total Reads] = SUM(total_logical_reads),

  [Execution Count] = SUM(qs.execution_count),

  [DatabaseName] = DB_NAME(qt.dbid)

  FROM sys.dm_exec_query_stats qs

  CROSS APPLY sys.dm_exec_sql_text(qs.sql_handle) as qt

  GROUP BY DB_NAME(qt.dbid)

  ORDER BY [Total Reads] DESC

when this procedure returns a NULL for the database name what thoughts should be raised in a DBA's mind? (Select all that apply.)

Choose three of the answers below:

1. Query plans are not being reused.

2. A NULL database name is never returned.

3. Code is not being reused.

4. Potential for security problems.

Answer:

1. Query plans are not being reused.
3. Code is not being reused.
4. Potential for security problems.

Explanation:

If you read the article just below Figure 2, there is mention that when this query returns NULL for the database name, there is code not being reused, meaning query plans aren't being re-used, and potentially there could be security issues.

Ref: **http://msdn.microsoft.com/en-us/magazine/cc164174.asp** - Presume permission since it appears in a publicly sold magazine

Question 81

What type of database is used on this site?

Choose one of the answers below:

1. Oracle

2. MS SQL Server 2000

3. MySQL

4. MS SQL Server 2005

5. MS Access

Answer:

4. MS SQL Server 2005

Explanation:

Of course the background of this site is MS SQL Server 2005! After running SQL Server 2000 for 6 years, the database was upgraded to SQL Server 2005 in September 2007.

Question 82

Assuming you've taken these steps to prevent SQL Injection:

Replace single-quote ' with double-single-quote "

Check for Select, Update, Delete

What happens if your web page runs into this at the end of the URL:

/YourPage.asp?account=1;declare @a varchar(1000);set @a=cast(0x73656C656374206E616D652066726F6D207379732E6461746162617365733B as varchar(1000));exec(@a)

And runs that in a dynamic SQL command in SQL Server 2005?

Choose one of the answers below:

1. Error Message "Syntax error near '0x736...'"

2. Nothing

3. A list of all the databases on your server

Answer:

3. A list of all the databases on your server

Explanation:

This is a currently common SQL injection attack. If the web page does not use stored procedures, but instead uses dynamic SQL, this is a valid SQL 2005 command (there are versions for SQL 2000), and might execute.

cast(0x73656C656374206E616D652066726F6D207379732E6461746162617365733B as varchar(1000)) resolves to "select name from sys.databases;".

With Varchar(max) and Varbinary(max), much more complex commands can be issued.

Question 83

When writing a Common Table Expression, which is the proper order of the clauses? Assume the ORDER BY, GROUP BY, and SELECT clauses apply to the outer query, not the query used to define the CTE.

Choose one of the answers below:

1. SELECT, WITH, GROUP BY, ORDER BY

2. WITH, SELECT, ORDER BY, GROUP BY

3. WITH, SELECT, GROUP BY, ORDER BY

4. GROUP BY, SELECT, ORDER BY, WITH

Answer:

3. WITH, SELECT, GROUP BY, ORDER BY

Explanation:

When creating a Common Table Expression, the WITH clause is first and preceeds the SELECT clause of the query. GROUP BY, if needed, is before ORDER BY, in a SELECT query. Note that the CTE contains it's own query inside parenthesis, all of which is a part of the WITH clause and there can be multiple queries for separate CTEs that are being built.

Ref: WITH - **http://msdn.microsoft.com/en-us/library/ms175972.aspx**
Using Common Table Expressions - **http://msdn.microsoft.com/en-us/library/ms190766.aspx**

Question 84

In creating a query that will be used in Query Notification, how are the SET options determined for the query?

Choose one of the answers below:

1. The client defaults are used (whatever they are)

2. The client's current settings are used (whatever they are)

3. The server's defaults are used (whatever they are)

4. A specific group of SET options are required on the client.

Answer:

4. A specific group of SET options are required on the client.

Explanation:

When building a query for query notification, a specific set of SET option setttings must be on the client's connection. specifically they are:

ANSI_NULLS ON
ANSI_PADDING ON
ANSI_WARNINGS ON
CONCAT_NULL_YIELDS_NULL ON
QUOTED_IDENTIFIER ON
NUMERIC_ROUNDABORT OFF
ARITHABORT ON

Ref: Creating a Query for Notification -
http://msdn.microsoft.com/en-us/library/ms181122.aspx

Question 85

Which of these is an invalid Query Notification query?

Choose two of the answers below:

1. SELECT * from Customers

2. SELECT Customers.*, Orders.OrderID FROM Customers Inner Join Orders on Customer.CustomerID = Orders.CustomerID

3. SELECT CustomerID, CustomerName from Customers

4. SELECT SUM(Orders.OrderTotal) FROM Orders

Answer:

1. SELECT * from Customers
4. SELECT SUM(Orders.OrderTotal) FROM Orders

Explanation:

There are a number of restrictions when dealing with Query Notification queries and they can be viewed in the reference below. Specifically in the answers, a SELECT * is invalid, as is an unnamed column. The SUM() column does not have an alias, so it is unnamed.

Ref: Creating a Query for Notification - **http://msdn.microsoft.com/en-us/library/ms181122.aspx**

Question 86

In SQL Server 2005, which is the preferred way of updating data in a TEXT column?

Choose one of the answers below:

1. UPDATETEXT ...

2. UPDATE ... SET [col] .WRITE ...

3. WRITETEXT ...

Answer:

2. UPDATE ... SET [col] .WRITE ...

Explanation:

The UPDATETEXT and WRITETEXT commands are being deprecated and will be removed in future versions, so the UPDATE with .WRITE option should be used in SQL Server 2005 and later.

Ref: UPDATE - **http://msdn.microsoft.com/en-us/library/ms177523.aspx**
WRITETEXT - **http://msdn.microsoft.com/en-us/library/ms186838.aspx**
UPDATETEXT - **http://msdn.microsoft.com/en-us/library/ms189466.aspx**

Question 87

What kind of things do you expect on Friday the 13th? (select all that apply).

Choose two of the answers below:

1. A promotion

2. A corrupt database

3. A bonus

4. Code checked in on the 12th has mysteriously disappeared.

Answer:

2. A corrupt database
4. Code checked in on the 12th has mysteriously disappeared.

Explanation:

Friday the 13th is typically seen as a day of bad luck, so you'd expect bad things to happen.

Hopefully all of you are having a great day.

Question 88

Which of the following items can be used to end a WAITFOR statement in SQL Server 2005?

Choose four of the answers below:

1. A specific time

2. An elapsed period of time

3. A message in a Service Broker queue

4. A timeout

Answer:

1. A specific time
2. An elapsed period of time
3. A message in a Service Broker queue
4. A timeout

Explanation:

All of these can actually end a WAITFOR statement. You can pick a particular time or an amount of time that elapses in the statement. You can also specify that the WAITFOR ends when a message is received in a Service Broker queue, or a timeout passes in waiting for that message.

Ref: Using WAITFOR - **http://msdn.microsoft.com/en-us/library/ms188253.aspx**

Question 89

If you open a cursor, which of these will allow you to get a count of the number of rows in the cursor? (select all that apply)

Choose three of the answers below:

      1.   sp_cursor_list

      2.   sp_describe_cursor

      3.   sp_describe_cursor_columns

      4.   @@cursor_rows

Answer:

1. sp_cursor_list
2. sp_describe_cursor
4. @@cursor_rows

Explanation:

All of these items except sp_describe cursor columns will allow you to determine the number of rows in some cursors, subject to restrictions. The @@Cursor_rows requires a non-dynamic cursor.

Ref: sp_cursor_list - **http://msdn.microsoft.com/en-us/library/ms186256.aspx**
sp_describe_cursor - **http://msdn.microsoft.com/en-us/library/ms173806.aspx**
sp_describe_cursor_columns - **http://msdn.microsoft.com/en-us/library/ms182755.aspx**
@@cursor_rows - **http://msdn.microsoft.com/en-us/library/ms176044.aspx**

Question 90

Assuming that I have the following values in the
TimeGroup table (value1, value2, value3, value4),
what does this query return?

  if 'Value1' < any (select column1 from
TimeGROUP)

 select 1

else

 select 0

Choose one of the answers below:

      1.   1

      2.   0

Answer:

1. 1

Explanation:

This query checks the value given against the subquery by applying the "ANY" keyword to the operation. If any value meets these criteria, then TRUE is returned to the IF statement and it is true in this case since "VALUE1" was given in the question.

Ref: ANY - **http://msdn.microsoft.com/en-us/library/ms175064.aspx**

Question 91

Assuming that I have the following values in the
TimeGroup table, not case sensitive, (value1, value2,
value3, value4), what does this query return?

 if 'value1' < all (select column1 from TimeGroup)

 select 1

else

 select 0

Choose one of the answers below:

1. 1

2. 0

Answer:

2. 0

Explanation:

This query checks the value given against the subquery by applying the "ALL" keyword to the operation. If all of the values returned meet these criteria, then TRUE is returned to the IF statement and it is false in this case since "VALUE1" was given in the question and that is not less than "value1". If A >= would return true.

Question 92

If you ALTER ASSEMBLY for one of your CLR objects and set the visibility to OFF, what does this imply?

Choose one of the answers below:

1. No new objects can be created against the assembly

2. This assembly is only intended to be called by other assemblies

3. The assembly is disabled and all objects calling it return an error.

4. Reflection will not work with this assembly.

Answer:

2. This assembly is only intended to be called by other assemblies

Explanation:

The visibility property determines if the assembly can be called by other objects (stored procedures, functions, etc.) or only from other assemblies. OFF implies only other assemblies will call it. If you have objects referencing this assembly, the visibility cannot be changed.

Ref: ALTER ASSEMBLY -
http://msdn.microsoft.com/en-us/library/ms186711.aspx

Question 93

You have a table with EmpName and DateOfLeaving columns. The EmpName column is mandatory, but DateOfleaving will have null value for those employees who have not left the company. The question is to have list off all employees with the employees with DateOfLeaving coming last and all others sorted ascending order of date of leaving, Name sorted in ascending order for each group. Consider the Example:

Table: Employees
EmpName DateOfLeaving Abc   10 Oct 1999 Bcd 11 Nov 1998 Ccd   null Dcd   10 Aug 2000 Eed null

The solution should be:
EmpName DateOfLeaving Bcd   11 Nov 1998 Abc 10 Oct 1999 Dcd   10 Aug 2000 Ccd   null Eed   null

Which query will produce this output? (select all that apply)

Choose one of the answers below:

1. Select EmpName, DateOfLeaving from Employees order by DateOfLeaving, EmpName asc

2. Select EmpName, DateOfLeaving from Employees order by isnull(DateOfLeaving,'10/10/9999'),EmpName asc

3. Select EmpName, DateOfLeaving from Employees order by DateOfLeaving desc, EmpName asc

Answer:

2. Select EmpName, DateOfLeaving from Employees order by isnull(DateOfLeaving,'10/10/9999'),EmpName asc

Explanation:

In SQL Server T-SQL, by default, a query takes null as first when the order is ascending (the default). So we just give some value of greater date in order by so that it will come at last.

Ref: ORDER BY -
http://msdn.microsoft.com/en-us/library/ms188385.aspx

Question 94

Does DBCC CHECKDB require space in tempdb?

Choose one of the answers below:

1. Yes

2. No, all activity is in the current database being checked.

Answer:

1. Yes

Explanation:

A number of structures are created in memory while running tempdb and these can spill into tempdb if space is needed. It is not guarenteed that tempdb will be used, but it is used by the CHECKDB process if required.

Ref: CHECKDB From Every Angle: Why would CHECKDB run out of space? - **http://www.sqlskills.com/blogs/paul/2007/11/06/CHECKDBFromEveryAngleWhyWouldCHECKDBRunOutOfSpace.aspx** (near the bottom)

Question 95

DECLARE @abc TABLE
(
A numeric(13,8),
B numeric(13,8),
C numeric(13,8)
) INSERT INTO @abc VALUES(1000,100,0)
UPDATE @abc
SET C= (A * B)

Question : What happened Now?

Choose one of the answers below:

1. Col C value updated to 100000

2. Col C Value updated to 1000

3. Col C Value updated to 100

4. Col C Value updated to 0

5. Error: Arithmetic overflow error converting numeric to data type numeric.

Answer:

5. Error: Arithmetic overflow error converting numeric to data type numeric.

Question 96

Database SnapShots are not allowed on which databases? (Check all that apply)

Choose three of the answers below:

1. SalesDB

2. master

3. tempdb

4. AdventureWorksDW

5. model

6. msdb

Answer:

2. master
3. tempdb
5. model

Explanation:

Database snapshots cannot be created on master, tempdb and model databases.

Ref: Limitations on Database Snapshots - **http://technet.microsoft.com/en-us/library/ms189940.aspx**

Question 97

You have a default standard SQL 2005 SP2 server. There is a table BigTable (col1 varchar(50)) with 10,000 rows. Which of the following statements are guaranteed to return 1000 rows? (select all that apply)

Choose two of the answers below:

1. select top 1000 col1 from bigtable

2. select col1 from bigtable tablesample system (1000 rows)

3. select top 10 percent col1 from bigtable

4. select col1 from bigtable tablesample system (10 percent)

Answer:

1. select top 1000 col1 from bigtable
3. select top 10 percent col1 from bigtable

Explanation:

TABLESAMPLE returns an approximate percentage of rows, even if a number of rows is specified. TOP will return the number of rows specified if that number of rows exist.

Ref: Limiting Result Sets by Using TABLESAMPLE - **http://technet.microsoft.com/en-us/library/ms189108.aspx**
Limiting Result Sets by Using TOP and PERCENT - **http://technet.microsoft.com/en-us/library/ms187043.aspx**

Question 98

You have a default standard SQL 2005 SP2 server.

There is a table BigTable (col1 varchar(50)) with 10,000 rows.

How many rows does the following statement return?

  select col1 from bigtable tablesample system (10 percent)

Choose one of the answers below:

1. 10

2. 1000

3. 10000

4. impossible to determine

Answer:

4. impossible to determine

Explanation:

TABLESAMPLE returns an approximate percentage of rows, even if a number of rows is specified. This is used to get a sample of data from large rows and does not guarentee a number of rows or a random sample.

Ref: Limiting Result Sets Using TABLESAMPLE - **http://technet.microsoft.com/en-us/library/ms189108.aspx**

Question 99

Since SQL Server is mostly developed in the US, it's a holiday, and the editor lives in Denver, who were the main characters in the movie *Independence Day*? An easy 10 points for you.

Choose two of the answers below:

1. Will Smith

2. Denzel Washington

3. Dennis Quaid

4. Jeff Goldblum

Answer:

1. Will Smith
4. Jeff Goldblum

Explanation:

Independence Day is a great science fiction, adventure movie about aliens invading the Earth and us fighting back on July 4th, Independence Day in the US. Will Smith and Jeff Goldblum play a fighter pilot and TV engineer respectively. Recommended for this weekend if you haven't seen it (or even if you have).
Ref: Independence Day -
http://www.imdb.com/title/tt0116629/

Question 100

How can you move data files in SQL Server 2005 from one drive to another? (Check all that apply)

Choose three of the answers below:

1. Use sp_detach_db and sp_attach_db

2. ALTER DATABASE

3. Shut down the instance, move the files to a new drive, restart the instance with the -D parameter that specifices the database name and new path departed by a colon.

4. Backup the database, drop it, and restore it using the WITH MOVE option.

Answer:

1. Use sp_detach_db and sp_attach_db
2. ALTER DATABASE
4. Backup the database, drop it, and restore it using the WITH MOVE option.

Explanation:

There are two basic ways of moving data files in SQL Server 2005. You can detach the files, copy them to the new location, and then attach them back. You can also use the ALTER DATABASE command with the MODIFY FILE options. You can also backup the database, drop it, and restore using the new location.

Ref: Moving User Databases - **http://msdn.microsoft.com/en-us/library/ms345483.aspx**

SQL Server, .NET and Exchange Tools
from **Red Gate Software**

SQL Backup™ Pro $795

Compress, encrypt, and strengthen SQL Server backups

↗ Compress SQL Server database backups by up to 95% for faster, smaller backups

↗ Protect your data with up to 256-bit AES encryption

↗ Strengthen your backups with network resilience to enable a fault-tolerant transfer of backups across flaky networks

↗ Control your backup activities through an intuitive interface, with powerful job management and an interactive timeline

> "With version 6 introducing a fourth level of compression and network resilience, SQL Backup will be a REAL boost to any DBA."
> **Jonathan Allen** Senior Database Administrator

SQL HyperBac™ $795

Silent compression for faster, smaller SQL Server backups

↗ Silently compress SQL Server backups by up to 95%

↗ Works seamlessly with T-SQL commands and requires no changes to existing backup techniques

↗ Protect your data with 256-bit AES encryption

↗ Back up to .zip for restores to any server, free from proprietary formats

> "The beauty of SQL HyperBac is that you do not need to alter what you are doing. Just install the software, configure the service, and you are essentially done; no messy re-writes of backup jobs. The backup time is also significantly reduced, along with the actual size of the backup file."
> **Doug Johns** MCDBA

Visit **www.red-gate.com** for a 14-day, free trial

SQL Virtual Restore™ $495

Rapidly mount live, fully functional databases direct from backups

↗ Turn backups into live databases for quick and easy access to data, without requiring a physical restore

↗ Live databases mounted by SQL Virtual Restore require significantly less storage space than a regular physical restore

↗ Recreate a fully functional database - databases mounted with SQL Virtual Restore support both read/write operations

↗ Perform smart object level recovery - SQL Virtual Restore is ACID compliant and gives you access to full, transactionally consistent data, with all objects visible and available

↗ Verify your backups - run DBCC CHECKDB against databases mounted by SQL Virtual Restore, without requiring the space and time for a full restore

> **"SQL Virtual Restore offers several important benefits to DBAs that a standard restore can't provide: substantial space savings, and substantial restore time savings."**
> **Brad McGehee** Director of DBA Education, Red Gate Software

SQL Storage Compress™ $1,595

Silent data compression to optimize SQL Server storage

↗ Reduce the storage footprint of live SQL Server databases by up to 90% to save on space and hardware costs

↗ Works seamlessly with compressed files – databases compressed with SQL Storage Compress are live and fully functional

↗ Integrates seamlessly with SQL Server and does not require any configuration changes

↗ Protect the data in your live databases with 256-bit AES encryption

Visit **www.red-gate.com** for a 14-day, free trial

SQL Response™ $495

Monitors SQL Servers, with alerts and diagnostic data

↗   Intuitive interface to enable easy SQL Server monitoring, configuration, and analysis

↗   Email alerts as soon as problems arise

↗   Investigate long-running queries, SQL deadlocks, blocked processes, and more, to resolve problems sooner

↗   No installation of components on your SQL Servers

↗   Fast, simple installation and administration

> **"SQL Response enables you to monitor, get alerted, and respond to SQL problems before they start, in an easy-to-navigate, user-friendly, and visually precise way, with drill-down detail where you need it most."**
>
> **H John B Manderson** President and Principal Consultant, Wireless Ventures Ltd

Coming soon! SQL Response™ v2

SQL Response v2 will save you time and help you ensure your servers are running smoothly.

On call and out of the office? SQL Response v2's new web UI means you can even check your server health and performance on the go - with most mobile devices.

New features include:

↗   Intuitive overviews at global, machine, SQL Server and database levels for up-to-the minute performance data

↗   Intelligent SQL Server alerts via email and an alert inbox in the UI notify you as soon as problems arise

↗   Historical data, so you can quickly go back in time to identify the source of a problem

Visit **www.red-gate.com** for a 14-day, free trial

SQL Compare Pro® $595

Compare and synchronize SQL Server database schemas

↗ Automate database comparisons, and synchronize your databases
↗ Simple, easy to use, 100% accurate
↗ Save hours of tedious work, and eliminate manual scripting errors
↗ Work with live databases, snapshots, script files, or backups

SQL Data Compare Pro™ $595

Compare and synchronize SQL Server database contents

↗ Compare your database contents
↗ Automatically synchronize your data
↗ Row-level data restore
↗ Compare to scripts, backups, or live databases

Visit **www.red-gate.com** for a 14-day, free trial

SQL Toolbelt™ $1,995

The essential SQL Server tools for
database professionals

You can buy our acclaimed SQL Server tools individually or
bundled. Our most popular deal is the SQL Toolbelt: fourteen of
our SQL Server tools in a single installer, with **a combined value
of $5,930 but an actual price of $1,995**, a saving of 66%.

Fully compatible with SQL Server 2000, 2005, and 2008.

SQL Toolbelt contains:

- ↗ **SQL Compare Pro**

- ↗ **SQL Data Compare Pro**

- ↗ **SQL Source Control**

- ↗ **SQL Backup Pro**

- ↗ **SQL Response**

- ↗ **SQL Prompt Pro**

- ↗ **SQL Data Generator**

- ↗ **SQL Doc**

- ↗ **SQL Dependency Tracker**

- ↗ **SQL Packager**

- ↗ **SQL Multi Script Unlimited**

- ↗ **SQL Refactor**

- ↗ **SQL Comparison SDK**

- ↗ **SQL Object Level Recovery Native**

> "The SQL Toolbelt provides tools
> that database developers, as well
> as DBAs, should not live without."
> **William Van Orden** Senior Database Developer,
> Lockheed Martin

Visit **www.red-gate.com** for a 14-day, free trial

ANTS Memory Profiler™ $495

Profile the memory usage of your C# and VB.NET applications

↗ Locate memory leaks within minutes

↗ Optimize applications with high memory usage

↗ Get clear, meaningful profiling results, for easy interpretation of your data

↗ Profile any .NET application, including ASP.NET web applications

> "Freaking sweet! We have a known memory leak that took me about four hours to find using our current tool, so I fired up ANTS Memory Profiler and went at it like I didn't know the leak existed. Not only did I come to the conclusion much faster, but I found another one!"
>
> **Aaron Smith** IT Manager, R.C. Systems Inc.

ANTS Performance Profiler™ from $395

Profile and boost the performance of your .NET code

↗ Speed up the performance of your .NET applications

↗ Identify performance bottlenecks in minutes

↗ Drill down to slow lines of code, thanks to line-level code timings

↗ Profile any .NET application, including ASP.NET web applications

> "Thanks to ANTS Performance Profiler, we were able to discover a performance hit in our serialization of XML that was fixed for a 10x performance increase."
>
> **Garret Spargo** Product Manager, AFHCAN

Visit **www.red-gate.com** for a 14-day, free trial

.NET Reflector ®   **Free**

Explore, browse, and analyze .NET assemblies

↗ View, navigate, and search through the class hierarchies of .NET assemblies, even if you don't have the source code for them

↗ Decompile and analyze .NET assemblies in C#, Visual Basic and IL

↗ Understand the relationships between classes and methods

↗ Check that your code has been correctly obfuscated before release

.NET Reflector Pro®   **$195**

Step into decompiled assemblies whilst debugging in Visual Studio

↗ Integrates the power of .NET Reflector into Visual Studio

↗ Decompile third-party assemblies from within VS

↗ Step through decompiled assemblies and use all the debugging techniques you would use on your own code

SmartAssembly™   from **$795**

.NET obfuscator and automated error reporting

↗ First-rate .NET obfuscator: obfuscate your .NET code and protect your application

↗ Automated error reporting: get a complete state of your program when it crashes (including the values of all local variables)

↗ Improve the quality of your software by fixing the most recurrent issues

Visit **www.red-gate.com** for a 14-day, free trial

Exchange Server Archiver $25 per mailbox
Email archiving software for Exchange   (200 mailboxes)

↗   Email archiving for Exchange Server

↗   Reduce size of information store – no more PSTs/mailbox quotas

↗   Archive only the mailboxes you want to

↗   Exchange, Outlook, and OWA 2003, 2007, and 2010 supported

↗   Transparent end-user experience

> **"Exchange Server Archiver is almost 100% invisible
> to Outlook end-users. The tool is simple to install and
> manage. This, combined with the ability to set up different
> rules depending on user mailbox, makes the system easy
> to configure for all types of situations. I'd recommend this
> product to anyone who needs to archive exchange email."**
> **Matthew Studer** Riverside Radiology Associates

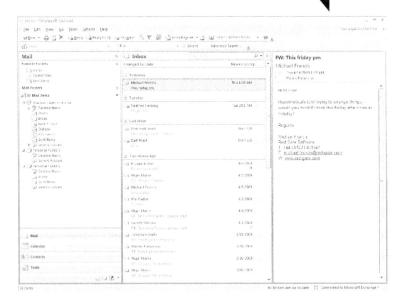

Visit **www.red-gate.com** for a 14-day, free trial

The Red Gate Guide to SQL Server Team Development

Phil Factor, Grant Fritchey and Mladen Prajdić

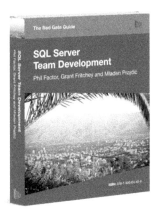

The Red Gate Guide to SQL Server Team Development describes how to develop database applications in a team environment. It shows how to solve many of the problems that the team will face when writing, documenting, and testing database code, such as code quality, maintainability, source control, static code analysis, code reuse, revision and refactoring.

ISBN: 978-1-906434-50-2
Published: November 2010

Defensive Database Programming

Alex Kuznetsov

Inside this book, you will find dozens of practical, defensive programming techniques that will improve the quality of your T-SQL code and increase its resilience and robustness.

ISBN: 978-1-906434-49-6
Published: June 2010

Brad's Sure Guide to
SQL Server Maintenance Plans
Brad McGehee

Brad's Sure Guide to Maintenance Plans shows you how to use the Maintenance Plan Wizard and Designer to configure and schedule eleven core database maintenance tasks, ranging from integrity checks, to database backups, to index reorganizations and rebuilds.

ISBN: 78-1-906434-34-2
Published: December 2009

SQL Server Tacklebox
Rodney Landrum

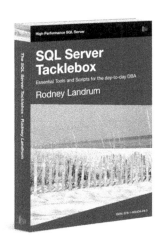

As a DBA, how well prepared are you to tackle "monsters" such as backup failure due to lack of disk space, or locking and blocking that is preventing critical business processes from running, or data corruption due to a power failure in the disk subsystem? If you have any hesitation in your answers to these questions, then Rodney Landrum's SQL Server Tacklebox is a must-read.

ISBN: 978-1-906434-25-0
Published: August 2009

www.ingramcontent.com/pod-product-compliance
Lightning Source LLC
LaVergne TN
LVHW022310060326
832902LV00020B/3370